William Graham (signature)

Terra Incognita:
Poetical Works

William Graham
2007

Text © William Graham 2007.

All rights reserved. No part of this book may be reproduced in any form or by any means, electronic or mechanical, including photocopying, recording or any information retrieval system, without prior permission in writing from the publishers.

ISBN-10: 1-4196-7625-3
EAN13: 978-1-4196-7625-3

Interior formatting/cover design by
Rend Graphics 2007
www.rendgraphics.com

Published by:
BookSurge Publishing
www.booksurge.com

To order additional copies, please visit:
www.amazon.com

To All People Who Explore

ಬಂಡ

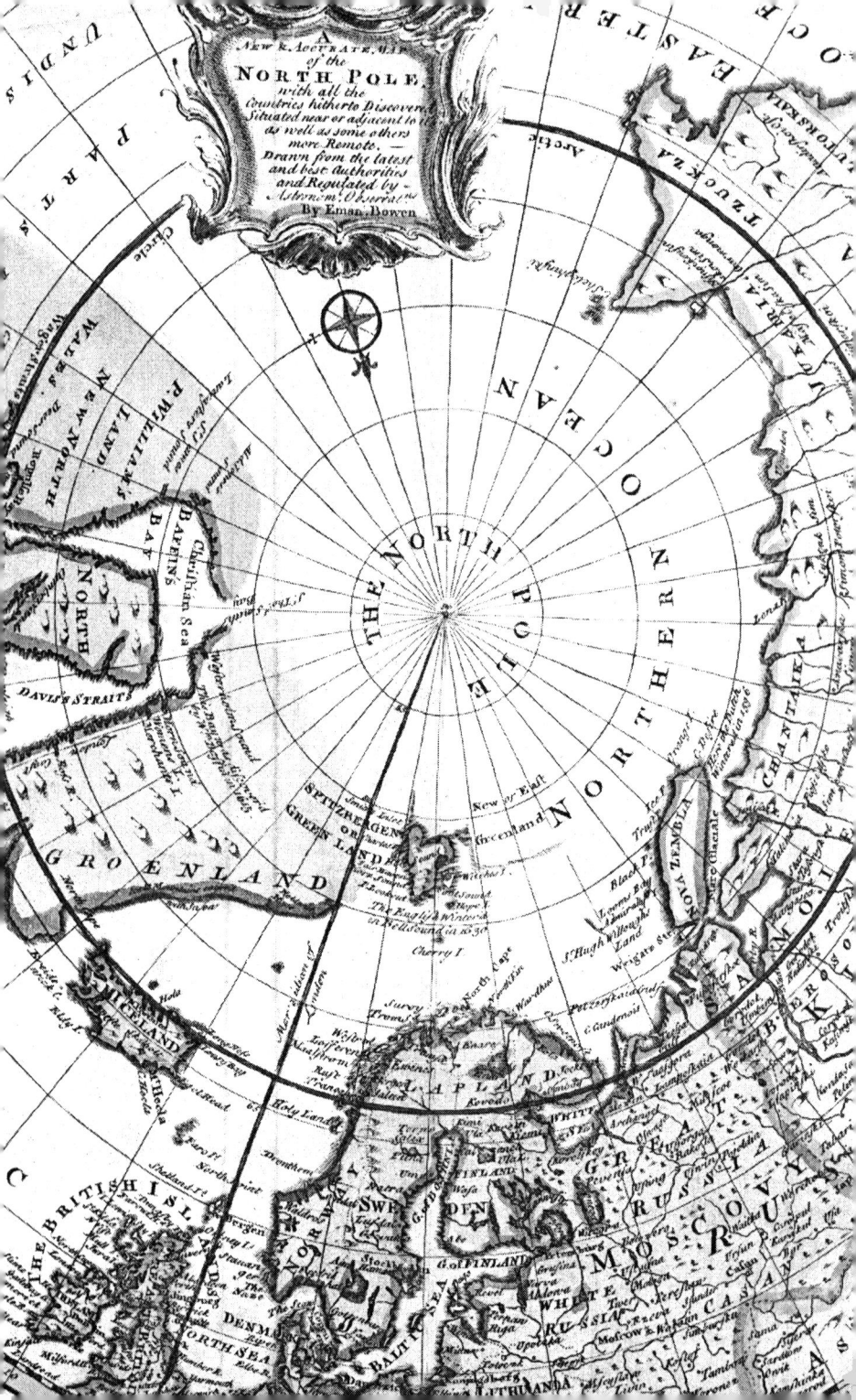

Terra Incognita

From our digital summit
We look down arrogantly
On the fools who believed
That the world was flat;
Who feared giant dragons
Rising from the seas.
We cannot remember a time
When people lived and died
Where they were born.
But our reach has exceeded
Our ability to grasp.
Everything is known, but little understood.

Invitation to the Dance

The invitation read "Spring Attire"—
Warm yellows and a touch of dark green.
The guests arrived early and with panache.
They entered the room like lightning bolts—
High voltage and cracks of noise.
Just when the soirée was in full gear,
An uninvited guest waltzed in and took a seat.
He was not adhering to the dress code.
His whites and cool grays were so last season.
He was asked politely to leave without
Causing a scene, but he would not be moved.
He lingered and ordered a few drinks on the rocks.
His icy demeanor turned some heads.
Eventually, he departed with a
Granite sneer and a dismissive
Flick of the wrist, as if telling
Everyone that he would be back.
The band leader called for blue music,
And everyone swayed to the warm tunes.

The Promise

Her promise hovered in air like a bee
Doing reconnaissance on a flower.
Would she keep her word to her first lover,
Or choose her second: a man of the sea?

The first waited by a lakeside lookout,
Entranced by eagles' airy dalliances
Under a sky bleeding blue. Perchance
She lost her way, he thought, as the sun went out.

He tramped back through the monastic forest.
That she left—he would let no one suggest.

Sunday Services

I could hear the clear Sunday bells ringing
At the church with ivory clapboards.
My service began at dawn with singing
Birds in cedars. Choral harmonies soared

Above the trees. No hymnal was required.
When it came time for the sermon, I saw
The mount where I would rest my old bones, tired
From the ascent. On the smooth rocks I paused

To hear the sacred text in the alpine
Wind. A holier mass I could not find.

New Year's Walk

The woods were wrapped in a white comforter.
The clock on the fireplace stretched to midnight.
In chilled moonlight, my lover's face glittered.
Ice-crusted trees bid us share the delight

Of celebrating the New Year. Out to
The woods we went, boots sinking in the snow.
We left dying embers behind to view
Stars welcoming us with their Arctic glow.

The Old Man on the Mountain

His knees creaked and burned as he ascended
The steep, rocky trail in the Green Mountains.
For years, his neighbors on him appended
The simple name of Old Man. It made sense

To everyone in the rural town.
Ten years before his wife fell to her death
On the same ridge to which he climbed at dawn.
He vowed that as long as he took a breath

He would make the trek and wait for Ella
To return to him. He declared to all
He would await the morning sun and a
Sign that she had risen after the fall.

Skipping Stones

I was a boy again on the quiet shore
Of Lake Champlain. The water was plate-glass
Still. I carefully gathered a store
Of smooth stones. Many mournful hours have passed

Since I last skipped stones across its azure
Water. I counted the leaps with joyous
Abandon. The smell of pine was a cure
For my cares. Birds told me to reassess.

Northern Eden

When he has grown weary of adult pursuits
And striving to acquire what he does not need,
He alights from his dreary cell for the routes
That will take him to where nothing is decreed.

He rambles along rocky knife-edge ridges
Where gossamer clouds romance the jagged peaks.
There he finds life sweet, fulsome and unabridged.
He finds enduring wisdom where no one speaks.

Phantoms on the Shore

When November winds howl in from the north;
When brown leaves are covered with fallen snow;
Old-timers will implore you to go forth
To the cold lake to see its ghostly show.

A century ago on a day like this
The *Maple Leaf* was loaded with lumber,
Headed for Quebec in the fog and mist.
Tossed by the black waves, the captain did stare

At his crew and told them to save their lives.
He would remain alone on the ship.
They must escape—for their children and wives.
They defied him and stayed as the wind whipped

The sails to shreds. The ship began to sink
Under the cruel waves. Twenty good men lost.
Many a widow was made. "Do not blink
When you go to the shore. Look sharp across

The water. For there you will see phantoms—
Mothers young and old wailing in the dark,
Stretching their arms out for their men to come.
But from that ship the crew will never disembark."

Evening Wear

The sky cut a dashing figure in his dark coat,
Which had been hung on a tree's wet, drooping branches.
He passed by each farmhouse in green valleys remote
To tell dwellers that the stars are taking their stances

In the vaulted sky to display their mystery.
Distant ripening fields began to fade from view.
In stone houses, old people spoke of eternity,
Vowing not to weep as they bid this world adieu.

Night Storm

Branches slapped the siding.
Rain assaulted the glass.
I was never one for chiding
When a storm came to harass.

For I knew that the storm
Would wipe clean the sky.
By morning, what was brown and worn
Would be a piercing blue for all eyes.

Heathens

When the wind rattles the corn
On a dripping summer day,
The sound is sweet to those born
On the land and there chose to stay.

Their skin smells of the rich earth.
Their hands are scratched and punctured
By the day's hard work. Their mirth
Comes when they shed clothes and head

To the shore of a still lake
At high noon. After plunging in
Cool waters, they lie and bake
On the sand—souls free from sin.

Unforgiven

Father was not spoken about.
On that Grandpa Horace was clear.
A man who could not be devout
Was someone we could not revere.

Mother and her parents reared us
On a marginal dairy farm.
Schoolmates would whisper on the bus
About father. It caused no harm.

For we were taught not to listen
To gossip. We sat—eyes focused
Ahead—oblivious to them.
God says not to show animus.

We grew up strong in the green fields.
The black soil was our true father.
Our mother's love alone did yield
Children second to no other.

Country Advice

His gray stone house dates back generations.
It sits stoically on a small hill
Above lush pastures where cows get their fill.
He speaks after long deliberations.

She owns three hundred acres next to his.
A mystery writer from Chicago,
She seeks utopia—a pace that's slow.
Life's frantic missions she wants to dismiss.

He tends to his herd as did his father.
She hangs flower boxes from his windows.
On cool mornings, his thick arms are exposed.
She burrows deep under her comforter.

She learns that his wife lies in the graveyard.
Her husband lies with a model in Spain.
She walks across his fields in the rain
To ask him bluntly if he finds it hard

To be alone. He scratches his bald head
And wipes his nose on his wet sleeve. "You see—
The land is all. It keeps me company."
That night, she sobs softly in her warm bed.

Rural Route Four

Her family had owned the land for
Two hundred years. Pastures sloped
Gracefully into the thick forest that,
As a child, she thought must go all the
Way to China.

One by one her parents and siblings
Coughed their way into the ground,
Leaving her to patrol the property on
Her tree-stump legs.

She sold the land to a man with a
Bovine face. She kept only the farmhouse
And her vegetable garden.
New neighbors sprouted like dandelions
In the spring. The sounds of milking cows
Were replaced by the squeals of children
And the crack of baseball bats.

But the sounds began to fade as her posture
Began to bend like a sapling in a nor'easter.
The one activity she looked forward to was
Walking to her new mailbox by the gravel road

With the number fifty-nine painted on it in
Bold black letters. Rural Route Four was now
Called Sycamore Lane.

Sometimes the absent-minded postal carrier
Would leave other people's mail in her box.
She noticed that one man worked for the
University; another liked sports; a third didn't
Pay his bills on time.

In the pre-dawn fog, before the mini-vans
Clogged the serpentine road, she returned
The letters to their rightful owners. She
Decided that she liked having neighbors;
They led such interesting lives.

She sat daily in her kitchen and waited for the
Shuffle of feet on the gravel under her mailbox.
It was her favorite sound.

Last of the Mohicans

Floyd Morrison surveys his back pasture
On a sultry day when taking a breath
Feels like you are drowning. Entrepreneurs'
Sprawling developments had caused the death

Of many a verdant field. Floyd's neighbors
Had sold out to move to Carolina.
But he remains, seeing to his labors
Daily—enjoying aromas of a

Freshly cut field and an old cattle barn.
His movements are sure—timed to nature's clock.
Making good use of land is his chief concern.
He will not be flying south with the flock.

Bountiful Harvest

Words spring from the ground like garden flowers.
Rhymes hang down from heavy tree limbs like fruit.
I harvest what I can from lonely hours
Spent in my dogged poetic pursuit.

I search the green hills unfolding like hands.
I ramble through valleys until twilight,
Searching for verses to take from the land's
Riches before I disappear from sight.

Evening Ramble

The man and woman are smaller now
Than when they arrived in the Green
Mountains thirty years ago. The evening
Seems darker to them now, and cooler,
As they walk through an orchard,
Hearing a brook singing beyond the trees.
The last touch of sunlight strokes the
Peaks as they walk through the thickening
Shadows. They raised their son here so
That he would know trees do not grow
In city parks and that food does not come
From grocery stores. The smells, shapes
And rhythms of the land grew into them
Over time. The couple spies a flock of
Birds silhouetted against the last light
Of day and squeeze each other's hand.

Adirondack Chairs

The lakeside chairs are silent witnesses
To life's dramas. They perch stoically
And listen as a father reminisces
To his son about climbing that tall tree.

They do not weep as an aging mother
Tells her daughter that she soon will perish.
A man explains he has found another.
They hear the howls of the one once cherished.

With angled ease they invite all strangers
To imbibe in the views of the High Peaks.
They do not judge opinions expressed there.
True friends—they listen well but do not speak.

Maine Woods

The boulders flowed down the merciless trail
Like rough waves on a crumbling sea under
A startlingly blue sky. To my left
A moose crashed through trees with the subtlety
Of a bulldozer. Millinocket was far
Behind me—a starting point at dawn's break.
Katahdin's spine beckoned above a blue
Lake that reflected its hulking image.
The mid-morning air chilled like white wine
As I ascended on scraped hands and knees
Like a pilgrim at Lourdes. Strong summit winds
Whipped my skin. I steadied myself to gaze
At the sea of green beneath. I was cured.

There's Always a Winter

There's always a winter—it's the time for parting,
When memories freeze to the ground.

There's always a winter—it's no time for starting
To conjure up words profound.

There's always a winter—the time when you prepare
For empty, silent rooms.

There's always a winter—when you just stare;
For spring's return, you must not presume.

Acadia

The Maine coastline unravels like a
Green necklace from the summit of
Cadillac Mountain. The rocks are
Now heating under the October sun,
Whose rays I greeted as the nation's
Earliest dawn hours before. Hawks
Dance in the crystal sky like memories
Climbing and diving in my skull.
Hearty autumnal embraces can
Soothe any wearied brow.

Giverny

October air hung heavy with the smell
Of burning leaves. The hypnotic sky's spell
Caused time to cease for suave locals who dwell

In Monet's village. My second sojourn
To Giverny led me back to the warm
Gallery where Pascal's paintings adorned

The walls of his stone farm house. A giant
Nude of his soft wife beckoned new clients.
Her mouth was sensual and compliant.

Pascal recognized me—an American
Who adored Monet and ignored Cézanne.
He placed a glass of white wine in my hand

And showed me his latest oils and sketches.
A drawing of a mother who stretches
Out her white hand to her young son catches

The essence of a mournful departure.
Their sad separation forever captured—
Frozen in the black frame that I procured.

Fire People

The fire people of Tierra del Fuego
Disappeared under the fog and snow.
Bullets and disease spelled their doom.
Their bones lie restless in antipodean gloom.

Cold Feet

The sky screamed blue above a calm sea
That cradled an island sanctuary.
Her mother and grandmother before
Spoke of how its peace could restore
Her mind. Each day the pine island
Sent her an invitation. She would stand
At the shore gazing at the green pearl
As she had done since she was a girl.
But then she would turn her back,
Returning to chaos in the cul-de-sac.
Her despair hung like bats in a cave.
She received little; too much she gave.
If she kept this Dantean pace,
She would disappear without a trace.
She dipped her rough foot in the bay,
But stopped. The water's cold—another day.

Mother's Day

She had reached her level of incompetence
When she gave birth to her third child near Christmas.
Her body had been under siege
For six years—always yielding.
Her sacred bookcase had turned into Pompeii—
Caked in the ash of unused thoughts.
Silence—once a refuge—had become a refugee,
Inhabiting a room not her own.
She once was cooked; now she is raw.
Her senses were once smooth; now they are chafed.
As number three suckled on a winter's day,
January's light slanted across the floor like the
Angled blade of a guillotine.
She had hoped to live in an Age of Enlightenment,
But found instead the Dark Ages.
Her geometrical French garden had been
Consumed by an encroaching jungle—
Boiling with the smell of decay.
When her trinity had finally drifted to sleep,
She stroked the keys of her piano like a lover,
Waiting for the eruption of
Joy that had long been dormant.

Second Childhood

I can feel my mind shrinking
Like an old birthday balloon.
A brain once used for thinking
Has disappeared much too soon.

My profound conversations
Now start and end with children's
Triumphs and tribulations.
I can no longer pretend

That I know much world affairs.
Time is consumed by laundry
And searching for lost Teddy Bears.
My college history degree

Is not much use when talking
Of rashes and soccer games.
I wish that each dawn would bring
Something new, but sameness remains.

I head to hockey practice
And then to dance. A chauffeur
Is what I have become. Such
Bliss you can have. I want more.

Father's Day

He walks to his minivan in the dark
Before his wife and three children arise.
The third—a boy—had come as a surprise.
Their family planning was off the mark.

Now he and his wife are outnumbered three
To two. Daily family logistics
Require advanced degrees and statistics.
When one sleeps, two others scream like banshees.

He had expected picturesque tableaus—
Tossing balls in the park and pushing swings.
Now, he loses sleep over bills that cling
To him like barnacles. He must forego

Paternal pleasures for working two jobs
And scrounging wildly for handyman work
Like a hungry stray dog going berserk.
He greedily accepts changing door knobs.

He and his wife long for reviving sleep
And the time to be parents and not drill
Sergeants. But each day he must find the will
To slog on as his hairline backwards creeps.

Measuring Up

He was told his family pedigree
And his studies at university
Would guarantee his lasting legacy.

But in adulthood he came to realize
Connections alone would not make him wise.
Inadequacies could not be disguised.

As his siblings made marks in high finance,
The choices he made showed little brilliance.
He surrendered—embracing nonchalance.

Economics Lesson

Sister LaStante's sixth grade class was driven
By earthly desires, not heavenly ones.
In all of Saint Patrick's, no other nun
Placed more stock in learning instead of sin.

We all had our scholar bank balances—
Earned from excelling on quizzes and tests;
By winning world geography contests.
We poured over our learning finances

As diligently as fund managers.
Our achievement points defined who we were—
On whom her glowing praise she would confer.
Some of us were stars, others were loafers.

Not everyone there was a winner.
Her system did not make us all equal.
You got what you earned, or nothing at all.
It was all about: How do you compare?

No mushy self-esteem building was required
To teach us to work for what we desired.

Decomposition

When he looked into her eyes,
He could see her decomposing
And drifting down the street
Like ash from a smoked cigarette.
Rather than retrieve the debris,
He turned and left,
Figuring that an antiseptic rain
Would wash away the gray
Stain on the cement.

Taking Stock

I opened the cupboard of memory.
I found nothing there.
It used to be fully stocked, you see.
Now, it's cold and bare.

Others ask me what I once preferred.
I often have no answer.
Instead, I stare, saying not a word.
Remembrance I can no longer stir.

Alone, I gaze at the wall of night.
For a second, I see food and drink.
They vanish quickly; it's my daily plight.
Only empty shelves, and nothing more to think.

Ready to Wear

She puts on her coat of despair.
She has nothing else new to wear.
It suits her—as she kneels for prayer.

She cannot discard the garment.
It is an old birthday present.
A hand-me-down—no money spent.

First owned by Grandmother Eileen
Who waited on train tracks unseen
Until struck by the four fifteen.

Her mother then wore it for years,
Wrapping her delusions and fears
In a dark fabric, stained by tears.

She is resigned to bleak couture.
No returning it—she is sure.
She prays long and seeks to endure.

A newborn child she will not bear.
The coat must grow musty and tear
On her back. On this she will swear.

Guitar

The Hartford poet need not have been so profound.
The guitar's beauty is simple: its glorious sound.
Nuanced fingers tame the six strings and make them weep.
A precise hand slides along the frets and notes leap
Through the sharp air in the colors of blue and red.
We hear how the composer must have long suffered,
Waiting for one woman's tender, amorous touch.
The virtuoso translates his anguish with such
Understanding that he unlocks the loneliness
From the heavy notes with grace, sympathy and finesse.
When the final bars of the tragedy are played,
We have traveled with them from the light to the shade.

Limerick

There once was a man named George,
But not the hero from Valley Forge.
He led us to war.
Who knows what for?
And to the world he's now a scourge.

On Visiting Lincoln's Tomb

The country has turned deaf to your words;
As deaf as the stone in which you are entombed.
Your classical oratory no longer has the magic
To unite a fragmented country.
You are now a tourist attraction—competing
With water slides and rollercoasters.
Your wrinkled face and iconic beard sell products;
But your ideas are dried up and cracked like the
Soil on the plains of Illinois in August.
Your large house remains, but it has been
Subdivided into condos. Rest in peace.

State Fair

Baking dust hovers at my ankles.
Heat drips from the sky like popcorn butter.
My hands are sticky with cotton candy.
The acrid smell of manure drifts from
The ancient stone livestock barn
With its cement floors still wet from
The last flushing by a teenager from 4-H.
High-pitched squeals of faux fright
From riders on the Scrambler and
Tilt-A-Whirl mingle with enticements
From barkers to play games of skill
That I am destined to lose.

There is an enticing, tattered innocence
At the State Fair. It is like a spinster
Who continues to dress up for Sunday
Mass even though she no longer has
A chance to snag a fair-haired beau.
A State Fair is a ritual of low expectations.
I attend to remind myself that pleasure
Can be found spinning like a dervish
On a ride that has twenty coats of paint,
Or sitting in a grandstand watching the

Sun set over corn fields as rusty cars
Plow into each other in the mud.
As the sky turns dark; low clouds roll
In from the west; they reflect the multi-
Colored lights of the Midway. The heavens
Shimmer with the past.

Volunteer

While politicians snarl and bark,
I patrol in the heat and mud.
I don't want to see my wounds and my blood.
When I'm killed, I hope it will be dark.

In your living eyes belong
Tears of joy. Do not wail over my grave.
We will rendezvous again. I will be saved.
When I'm killed; do not mourn too long.

I will live on your lips until you die.
A short kiss is better than a long goodbye.

False Prophets

Pick your prophet—the story is the same.
Hearsay upon hearsay created their fame.
Faithful disciples scribbled in damp caves,
And then told lost souls how to be saved.
If you seek paradise through faith's aid,
Understand this: God and Heaven are man made.

Alternative Gods

The priest arrived to tell us all
That because of Adam were are prone to fall
Swiftly into sin. He bid us rejoice
In the name of the Lord. But his choice
Was too limiting for me.
Give me Nepture and the open sea.
Let me hear Pan piping his tunes.
Let Bacchus join me for a drink on lazy afternoons.
Introduce me to some Druids who dance
Around flames and find natural romance.
For salvation I will not pray.
I have other plans on Judgment Day.

Distant Relations

Eve lived in Eden says the good book.
But you might want to take another look.
For found in the wet sands north of Cape Town
Were footprints of an Eve of less renown.

Her genes—not those of the Edenite—
Shaped who we are—our gait, our face, our sight.
We cannot deny—whatever our race—
Our mother has an African face.

The Bishop Laments

No one can be holy without suffering.
That formula cannot be denied.
My temporal shell is abandoning me,
Like a tortoise lumbering to the sea.
One day I will reach the sea, but not today.
These tubes anchor me to my bed.
I have been asked to make a statement to the press.
But I have refused. They are like hyenas
Looking to nibble at the carcass of a wasted life.
Yes, "wasted" is the correct word, I must confess.
It is lamentable that I could not control
My predilections. We all eventually
Betray ourselves. I was my own Judas.
Those few fumbling attempts at affection
Are all people can talk about. They have
Forgotten my good works. I heard
That a street would have been named in my honor.
That is, before the revelations. I am glad that mother
Has gone. She could not have endured the humiliation.
I hear someone coming to adjust my medication.
Then I shall take communion. Few people visit me now.
But I still have the photo of the Pope and me taken
At Saint Peter's. I was a bishop of great eminence once.

Transcribing Faith

Proclaiming himself the new Muhammad,
Joseph Smith set up his revelations
Shop in upstate New York. Found with the dead
Remains of the Native American nations
Were golden plates from heaven that revealed
Holy truths. Smith sought scriveners
To whom he would dictate what was unsealed
For him by ancient prophets. A neighbor
Martin Harris mortgaged his farm to help
Smith with his task. Forsaking his wife,
He joined the Smiths, dedicating himself
To transcribing truths that Smith brought to life.
As Smith intoned through a wool blanket hung
From the ceiling, Harris wrote down the tales
Of Nephi—given voice by Smith's smooth tongue.
Harris' wife fumed when she learned details
Of her feckless husband's naïve toils.
She stole the precious pages and challenged
Smith to recreate each grand syllable.
Ingenious Smith told her that God arranged
For him to translate new plates, which angels
Returned then to heaven. Smith found others
To do Harris' work. The fool nonpareil

Left swiftly—to scribble there no further.
Smith produced more divine revelations
That turned into the dry Book of Mormon.
But his ego led to complications
And strife. It came to pas—he was gunned down.

Herculaneum

Merchants sold their wares under the blazing
Sun in Herculaneum. The stifling
August heat seared—merciless. Elite
Families retreated from the dusty streets
To cool themselves in waters from mountains
Beyond the horizon. Dazzling fountains
Bubbled behind thick walls of the rich.
A marble Hercules gazed from a niche
In the stone. His noble visage reminded
Bathers that deities must be honored.
The muscular god founded the city
After slaying Cacus with no pity.
Citizens enjoyed a safe, plush life—
Finding fortune and love with little strife.
Then the soaring peak Mount Vesuvius
Shattered the afternoon peace, spewing dust
And rocks into the heavens—the dark cloud
A stone pine tree, casting a thick death shroud
First on their coastal neighbors at Pompeii.
Herculaneum's people fled the bay
Before the ash filled their lungs and scalded
Their skin—or so history thought. Buried
For centuries and forgotten, citizens

Were found huddled in stone boat houses, squeezed
Tightly together in communal fear—
Burned to carbon—strangers and those held dear.
A mother clutched her two frightened children.
Beside her a woman held jewels given
To her by her last lover, who had fled.
Did they scream, pray, cry—or was nothing said?

Liberators

Commander Varus led weary Roman
Legions into the damp German forest.
Black rain poured from the low sky—an omen
Of doom some thought while preparing to rest.

That the Germans would yield to Roman force
Varus had no doubt. Barbarians will
Drop like deer. Let rain fall on man and horse;
It matters not, he thought, ready to kill.

But the Fates proved unkind. Rains did not cease.
Men and carts sank deep in the Rhineland muck,
As if being swallowed by a brown beast.
The Roman line stretched for miles. Roman luck

Would be tested. Sentries told Varus
They were surrounded. Barbarians attacked
In waves. For three bloody days, Germans pressed
The fight. Thirty thousand Romans were hacked

To death on their civilizing mission.
Noble Roman Varus fell on his sword.
His head returned after decapitation
To haunted Augustus from Teutoburg.

Fruitlands

They came to this serene and sequestered dell–
Picturesque in beauty far and near–
With forested hills undulating from the south and west,
To live from the fruits of the land.

Five adults and five children sought to live
In harmony with the primitive instincts of men.
The land awaited to be consecrated by the
Sober culture of the families.

The sought to live close to the bone.
They planted fruits and grain, and then
Retired to the library to nourish their souls.
Their lofty conversations in the drafty house

Continued through the New England night.
Their gardens were ignored in favor of philosophical
Flights, garnished by the generous consumption of
Bland bran crackers.

They sowed little and reaped less
As the sultry summer yielded to frigid Canadian breezes.
Women and children became cold and hungry.
Universal divinity did not keep them warm at night.

They decided to pack up their books and their
Transcendental routine and return the farm to Nature.

Mourning

Thirty-two shot dead
The cable news channels said.
Before their families learned
Of their fate, candles burned
Next to Teddy Bears on the grass.
Strangers mourned before one mass
Had been said, before one grave had been dug.
Flocks of reporters arrived to hug
The grieving relations, not to ask questions.
Well-groomed anchors had no intention
Of asking how or why,
But just to look baffled and share a cry.
Mourning became a national ritual.
Was vicarious victimization now taught in school?
A greater decency there is in privately bearing it.
Nothing to be gained from publicly sharing it.
Everyone scrambles to find deeper meaning.
But tragedy is random. We are Fate's plaything.

Death of Poetry

Poetry was once suitable
For all. But now it is inscrutable
Except for scholars in academia
Who can solve a poem's formula.
We used to have great voices in verse,
But now such art has been cursed
By poets who write for workshops
And writers' colonies instead of Pops
And Moms.   We need poetry that breathes
Once again. Otherwise, funeral wreathes
Might as well be placed on piles
Of verse that will be fuel for bond fires.

Antarctica

It has been two months since the ground
Became her home. The swelling of the dirt
Is gone now and green whiskers of grass have
Begun to grow. The carved granite stone stands
Solid—a frozen reminder that she
Will not return. I do not visit her now.
I have moved to the Northern Kingdom of Vermont—
To fifty acres purchased from my uncle.
I do not talk much now. Sometimes I yell
While walking in the woods just to ensure
That my vocal chords still work—they do.
I depart for Antarctica in three weeks.
I want to experience the most remote,
The driest, the highest, the coldest
Place on earth while I am still breathing.
As a child, I would turn the globe in my
Room upside down to stare at the white expanse.
I wondered if my blood would rush to my head
At the bottom of the world. Comical
Penguins were never the attraction though.
It was the land's absolute emptiness.
If I could exist in nothing, then I
Could tolerate anything—even death.

I dream of standing on an iceberg
And drifting off into the Roaring Forties.
I would touch the ice as pure as a child's thoughts,
And wait for the silence to begin.
For I have no need for words now—stillness
Will suffice—from the Northern Kingdom
To the southern seas. Syllables complicate.
I phrase my life in eternal pauses.

White

In Antarctica, senses are heightened.
Overwhelming whiteness does not frighten.
Whiteness embraces with cold tenderness.
I savor its emptiness *in extremis*.

Iceberg

She saw the block of frozen purity
Floating on the gray ocean and saw herself—
Cold, sharp, mostly hidden, drifting, alone.
Eventually, it would disappear and melt—
Out of sight of ship and shore.
Standing on the deck of a ship plowing
Through the southern Atlantic, her eyes
Remained riveted to the iceberg as the
Waves rocked her. She touched her frozen
Skin and thought of the day she too
Would merge once again with the water.

Cool Customer

The cool starkness of her face intrigued him.
Her chin looked as if it had been chiseled from
An iceberg—it was sharp and angular.
If you caressed it, you ran the risk of cutting
Your fingers. He decided that she was enough
Of a rare prize to explore. Remoteness attracts.

Aran Islands

The ferry crossed dark Galway Bay
Headed toward the Aran isles.
The wind blew cold and mean that day.
Time froze solid as we passed the miles.

On the shore, the tempest relaxed.
Soon my saunter became steady.
Near a stone wall, I followed tracks
To the cliff of the White Lady.

Brendan had told me the sad tale
Of a woman, shy and lonely,
Who loved a man who loved his ale.
But she was not his one and only.

Many lovers the man did boast,
But not the White Lady. He laughed
At her frail shape—called her a ghost.
In her small stone house, she passed

The years, not speaking to a soul.
On a wind-swept December night
She plunged into the sea. Mortal
Bonds broken—now free from her plight.

Islanders recount the legend
When winter storms drop from above,
Of a ghost who from the sea ascends,
Looking for someone dear to love.

Traders

They step on the northbound train at three,
Sipping beers and talking of tee times.
On many topics they all agree.
Number one: making money is no crime.

They converse loudly so all can hear,
Complaining of wives grown tired and old.
They won't accept spouses so austere.
They turn to flesh that is bought and sold.

Change in the Forecast

Her look bent my resolve like old branches
In a north wind, scattering lush memories
Like brittle leaves on the forest's hard floor.
Once scorched by her desire, the early autumn
Caught me by surprise. I should have known better
Than to have ventured outside with no coat.

Death in the Outback

Traffic had stopped on the third-degree-burned
Pavement in the broiling outback. We stayed
In our cars and listened as the radio
Told us that an accident had closed
The highway to Thredbo. Shadows impaled
The rough landscape. A bloated sun hung like
A carcass on the horizon. Traffic began
To crawl again like an uncomfortable
Conversation past the dissected wreckage.
Father and son killed—we learned. We all
Hoped to arrive at our destinations before dark.

Past Closed

Do not bother to pack clothes.
Do not put gas in your cars.
Do not be prone to suppose
That you can heal ancient scars.

The past's iron gates are closed.
Why recite: "Remember when?"
Why travel to be exposed
To this pain: "What might have been?"

La Salle (1643-1687)
Part 1: To Illinois and Back (1679-1680)

Born in old France and called René-Robert,
He took his vows and became a priest there.
But he renounced his holy bond to God,
Leaving manicured France for the roughshod,
Frigid land of "Kanata"—the "village"
In the Huron tongue. Migrants of courage
And greed crossed the ocean to find riches
In the forests, lakes and streams in breeches
That soon grew tattered and aromatic.
Some came to stay; some to find rewards quick
And leave. René-Robert, Sieur de La Salle,
Journeyed to "Kebec"—the place he would call
His home. He recognized that the life-blood
Of Kanata was beaver. Trade would flood
His coffers with coins—an earthly reward
More sustaining than serving the dear Lord.

He was savvy enough to know success
Depended on learning how to address
The Iroquois nation—Onondaga,
Mohawk, Oneida, Cayuga, Seneca.
Savages though they were, they knew the lands

Beyond the sun where La Salle would command
His enterprise in beaver and buffalo.
He gathered men and stores. He would follow
The path charted by Marquette and Jolliet.
Taking no chances, he packed both intellect
And guns as he left the land of narrow
Waters. Moving west, La Salle's band tramped slow
Through the demon forest, arriving at Fort
Frontenac—crude structure that would support
His explorations into the godless
Interior. He prayed that God would bless
His journey and forgive his moral failures.

On a boiling day, his crew dipped their oars
Into Lake Erie aboard *Le Griffon*.
Oars up, sails unfurled, they reached Lake Huron;
Then northward to Michilimackinac.
They stuck close to shore and avoided attacks
From natives who spied on them from the trees.
He stopped to wait for Henri de Tonti,
Whose small party was crossing Michigan
On foot. After a brief rest, they began
A canoe trip down the great lake. Behind
Them they left Le Griffon and crew to find
Their way back to Lake Huron. Never would
They see the fair ship or its sailors. Good
Men all lost forever—to a winter

Storm or ambush? The dark, unkind water

Has not revealed its secret. La Salle's men
Had their own tribulations on the plains
Of Illinois, where the Iroquois waged
War against many western tribes. They staged
Brutal assaults—killing, raping, burning
All who breathed in the villages. Knowing
That his survival was at risk, La Salle
Forged a tribal alliance to battle
And defeat the Iroquois. Running short
On supplies, brave La Salle slogged back to Fort
Frontenac, leaving Tonti at Fort Crèvecoeur
With hungry and frightened men, who abjured
Loyalty and decency. They destroyed
The small fort—fearing giant serpents that toyed
With their victims before eating them alive.
They fled into the wilderness and cried
In the night, swallowed by the raging dark.

Desperate, Tonti maintained the last spark
Of humanity, waiting for monsieur
To rescue him. La Salle returned and assured
Him that his great suffering was over.
Though financially ruined, he pledged there
To ragged Tonti that they would yet see
The great river called the Mississippi.

Part 2: Discovery and Death (1682-1687)

Resolute, La Salle reassembled his
Party—twenty-three Frenchmen strong. To this
He added eighteen Native Americans.
They packed their stout canoes full and began
A trek across the frontier to the river
Called Illinois, whose waters delivered
Them to the Mississippi. They floated down
Its muddy waters, past banks overgrown
With trees and thickets—the territory
Where the Chickasaw hunted their quarry,
Where Choctaw, Natchez, Coroas and Oumas
Followed their own ancient customs and laws.
As the natives gazed at the strange visages
Before them, they could not know the stage was
Already set for their elimination.

Months of deprivation turned to elation
For La Salle's men as they came to the mouth
Of the Mississippi, deep in the south
Of the land now called Louisiana
By La Salle to honor great King Louis and
His wife Anne. A fatal mistake La Salle
Would make on that delicious day. For all
Who sought to find the entrance to the river
Would be thwarted by math that would deliver
Them hundred of miles off course to the west—
Proving tragic for La Salle's next grand quest.

Two years after naming Louisiana,
La Salle sailed from France, prepared to land a
Group of three hundred intrepid colonists
Who would found a French village in the mists
Of the bayou. Problems plagued the party.
Pirates sunk one ship on the open sea.
With La Salle's poor calculations, the other
Three ships sailed past the river's mouth, farther
West to Texas, where one ship sank, a second
Ran aground. Undaunted, La Salle reckoned
That shelter was needed, so Fort Saint Louis
Was quickly built. Heat and bugs did not buoy
The spirits of the survivors. Scorpions
And poisonous snakes killed many daughters, sons,
Mothers and fathers. Three times eastward
They trekked to find the river—with no reward.
Their desperation spurred depravity.
Mutineers slaughtered people without mercy.
Never finding riches, La Salle instead
Faced Pierre Duhaut, who shot him stone dead.
The Karankawa killed those who remained.
All rescuers found was buzzing and blood stains.

Louisiana Purchase

The land La Salle proclaimed for king
And country was used as a chip
In a high-stakes game that would bring
The expanse into Jefferson's grip.

Fearing the sea mistress Britain,
Napoleon sold the territory
To the States—an historic bargain
That sowed the seeds of our glory.

Jefferson gave orders to Lewis
And Clark to explore the Missouri
And reach the Pacific. On this
Epic journey, these men would see

Grand sights of mountain ranges immense,
Grass plains stretching to infinity—
Untouched all and ready for commerce.
Toward the tribes, they showed honesty,

Courtesy and respect, ensuring
That they survived. Clark's tongue was straight.
Others would find the land alluring,
But these ambassadors chose to berate

The Sioux, Flatheads and Nez Percés
As less than human. A dark stain
They made with their disdain and curses.
They took the land as their domain.

Before Lewis and Clark, the west
Was wilderness—land of fantasy
And myth. Now the States were blessed
With a treasure—our manifest destiny.

The Leper

Perfumed flowers breathed on Koolau. The night
Was illuminated by bloated stars.
He clenched his misshapen claws, poised to fight
The white soldiers. Becoming a martyr
To native Hawaiians was not his goal.
He desired only to live free amid
The flower-choked gorges that stirred his soul—
The Kalalau Valley, where he hid.
Soldiers advanced through forest thick and slick.
Koolau was poised to defend sacred ground.
Crouching low, he fired with aim true and quick.
Then he vanished. Five dead soldiers were found.
  Never caught, he savored tropical skies.
  He died free, not exiled on Molokai.

The Goddess of Hawaii

Hina's long hair crashed around her brown face
Like winter waves on the shore. The daughter
Of Uli, the imposing sorceress,
Hina was known to all as the treasure

Of the island. Hakalanileo
Became enamored with her fresh beauty.
To take her as his wife—it must be so.
Uli warned: "Winds will snatch her. You will see."

As she bathed with her maidens, Hina
Was captured by Kaupeepee. To Maui
She was taken, leaving two sons and a
Grieving husband far behind. Kaupeepee's

Tenderness melted Hina's heart in time.
For fifteen years, Hakalanileo
Searched for her in vain. Her two sons vowed to find
Hina. In the strong fortress of Haupu

They found her. The warriors of Kana
And Niheu fought bravely and overran
Haupu. Kaupeepee died nobly with a
Spear through his heart. To the island

Of her birth she was returned. Through sad years,
Hina called for Kaupeepee through her tears.

Angry Gods

In your fiery grotto you reside.
Pele, you ask too much of your people.
You gorge on their offerings and decide
Who will live and whose hot blood you will spill.

People of Hawaii—why do you serve
Such rash, merciless gods? Kilauea's
Royals mock you with storms and steam. Preserve
Your dignity. From their tight grasp withdraw.

House of the Sun

I enter the crater of
Haleakala—the House
Of the Sun—where Maui
Snared the star as it slid
Across the Pacific sky.
The old Hawaiian gods
Are sleeping quietly now.
There is no wind, no insects, no birds—
Only the sound of my boots crunching
On the black and gray cinders.
I climb a cinder cone to survey
The blasted valley as it slides
Into the sea two miles below.
Nothing disturbs my reverie.
My face shows the signature of the sun.

Kelea the Surfer

Spoiled as a child, Kelea became
A wayward woman—capricious
And volatile—not one to be tamed.
Toward men she was suspicious.

She saved her passion for the waves.
A surf-board was her lover.
She would rather go to her grave
Than warmly embrace any other.

But marry she did the royal
Lo-Lale, who gave her brilliant pearls.
For many years Kelea was loyal.
She bore him three lovely island girls.

Every comfort was hers, but nowhere
Could she find contentment. To the sound
Of the surf she was drawn. So she did swear
To mount again the waves. Never was she found.

Silent Will

Silent Will lived in a slumping frame house
That overlooked Bonne Bay. A lobster man
He was—sullen, stoic, not one to grouse.
A Newfoundlander since his life began.

His face had been scoured by the raging sea.
Hands hung at his side like iron anchors.
The shore of the Rock was his family.
When his wife left him, there was no rancor.

She fled with the children for the good life
In Toronto. "They will have a future,"
She said, "Where there is less turmoil and strife."
He said goodbye and wished them good luck there.

He roamed the jagged coast in all weather,
Nodding silently to those he would pass.
When he and his old crew sat together,
They knew that to the Rock they would hold fast.

Compensation

A wall of darkness presses on windows,
Signaling autumn it is time to go.
Arctic winds strut through the village.
The lead actor has taken center stage.

No one in Rocky Harbour can be found.
Save for the crash of waves, silence holds ground.
The clouds then lift and the northern lights dance.
People emerge, awed by nature's trance.

Villagers may live in isolation,
But wild beauty provides compensation.

Wilderness Survival

She handles men like they are fish—
First she hooks them with beauty;
Then she guts them with panache.
She considers it her duty.

She spends nights at the Anchor Bar
Flirting with the men she detests.
Her days she treks with hikers far
Into the Newfoundland forests.

Men are so weak, she says each night
As she kicks them out of her bed.
She prefers peace after delight—
Not sweet memories in her head.

Her muscles are strong; body lean.
Her skin immune to Arctic cold.
She will survive with her cunning
Until she lies down to grow old.

Winter in Newfoundland

They waited behind ice-covered windows
For the doctor to come on his sled.
Their daughter had coughed blood on her white clothes.
They feared in a few hours she would be dead.

Across the frozen moonlit emptiness
A lone doctor from Saint Anthony came.
He could do nothing to ease her distress.
She passed silently—there would be no blame.

The doctor stayed for the funeral service.
He had no choice—a blizzard closed the town.
Of pain and suffering, none could be worse
Than seeing a child placed in the cold ground.

Northern Exposure

Rush hour consists of a large moose
Crossing a meadow of wild flowers under
An exquisite blue sky. The delicious
Aroma of pine caresses my urban snout.
I head towards a lake carved in the woods.
A ballet of light greets me as I sit
On the shore, breathing deep the soft silence.
Newfoundland will leave the lights on for ten
More hours for me to enjoy its summer pageant.

Barren

Like a fist shoved through the earth's skull,
The Tablelands squat brown and hard
In the angled light of a Newfoundland
Morning. It sneers at the welcoming
Green pines on the surrounding hills.
It disdains plants and scoffs at color.
It beckons only those who won't cry
After twisting an ankle or cutting a hand.
If you make it down from the Tablelands—
Legs screaming for mercy—then you have
Experienced the severe beauty of absence.

The Explorer

It was an indentation in the forest—
A shallow sanctuary surrounded by
Drooping trees that leaned toward
The west, as if pleading for the
Sun never to set. It was the place
Where I learned to explore. With the
Morning grass still wet, I tramped
Through the bushes, sat on a sandstone
Bench and read of exotic destinations
That I vowed someday to visit—
Places beyond the strangling hills
Of the Mississippi Valley. I obsessively
Read maps, lovingly charting the ragged
Coastline of Maine or scanning the thin
Dagger called Chile. I touched the white
Blotches at the top and bottom of a globe
And could feel my fingers growing cold.
I ran my hands across the blue and
Could smell tropical flowers on distant
Volcanic islands. The world did not
End at the eastern shore of the Mississippi.
I needed to see around and over. I did not
Want my bones to be planted in the

Dark soil on which I walked. I would
Find a ridge where I could always
Survey the horizon. I vowed that
Such a place I would seek. I am
Seeking still.

TERRA AUSTRALIS INCOGNITA

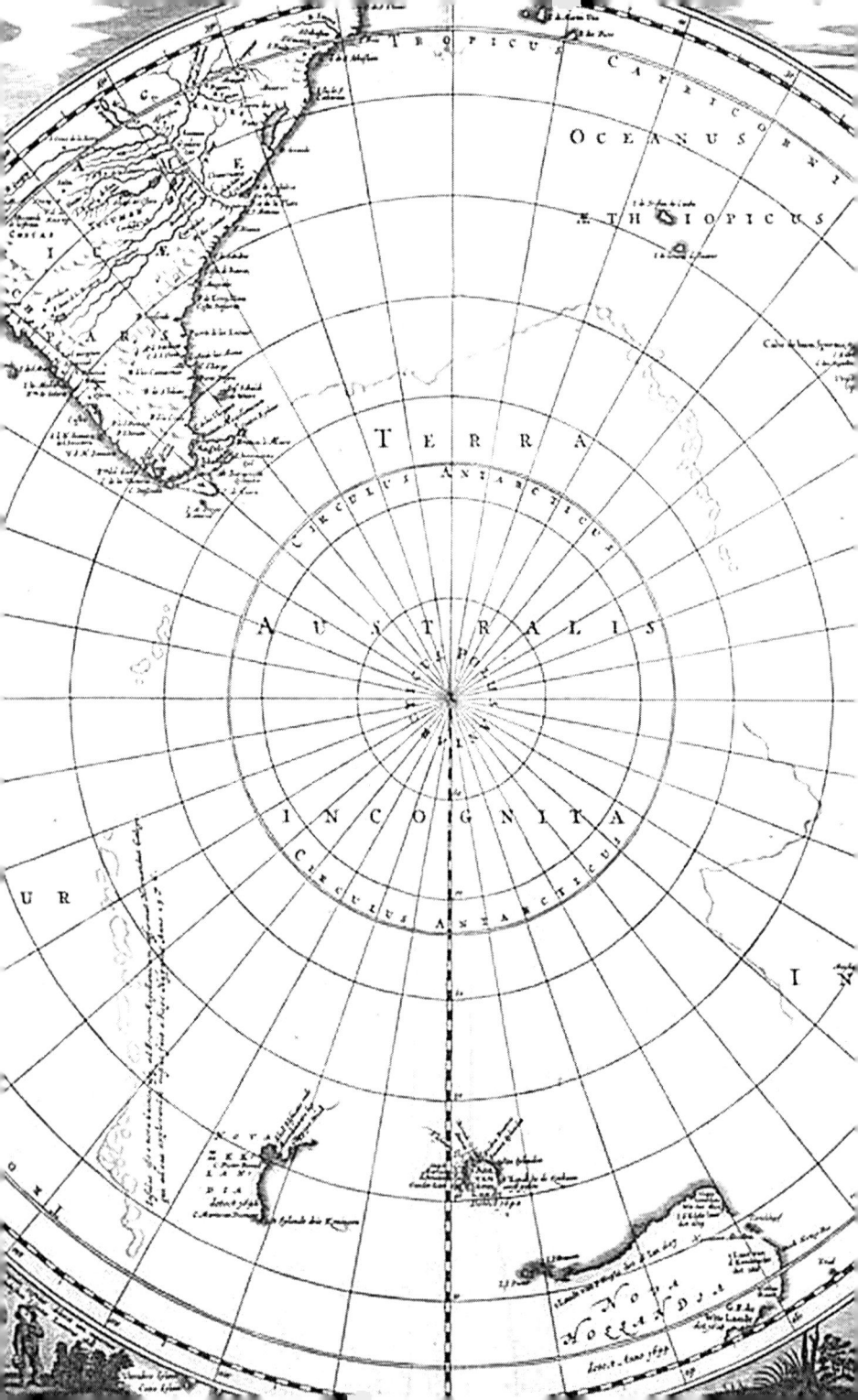